IMPERMANENCE

BY

SAM R GERAGHTY

VENEFICIA PUBLICATIONS UK

Text © Sam R Geraghty
Cover image © Alex Spence
art404.net

Editing & Typesetting ©
Veneficia Publications
UK February 2023
Veneficiapublications.com

To Rosa, Rachel, and Samuel

CONTENTS

INTRODUCTION

Poetry is my first love. I grew up like most children weaned on the nursery rhymes, as they lyrically told of history's more macabre events. And while many grow out of this, I confess I remained fascinated by the concept of stories told with rhythm and rhyme. I loved poetry of all forms, and then I experienced the Rubaiyat of Omar Khayyam, and the world of poetry had me hooked. I devoured Milton, Shelley, Rupert Brook et al. This was proper poetry, and then more recently came Sam R Geraghty's Dialectic. This was next level poetry, which I could only aspire to, yet could totally indulge myself in.

Sam R Geraghty writes, what I can only call, very polished, and very beautiful occult poetry, which is at times sublime. His words have a power; the power to capture the imagination and sing to the soul. Moreover, Dialectic is the soul, the soul of a poet. It is his hopes and dreams, his fears, and his longings. This is what gives Sam R Geraghty his edge.

This baring of the poetic soul is more apparent than ever in his latest work Impermanence. His collections are short, but they are powerful. Impermanence is at times raw, and unashamed in its approach. Nothing remains the same forever, everything changes – impermanence is that change. Existence is not permanent, its cycles are the impermanence, and impermanence is the journey, and the journey is ours. Beautifully written, wonderful in its deliverance and thought provoking throughout.

Impermanence is haunting, in it I recognise myself, the world around me, tales I have read, Gods I have known and my own sense of creation. I see chaos as much as I see beauty, and divine as a restlessness within. Impermanence is an echo of not only the past, but also the future. The humanity of the poet's soul is evident throughout, and my heart skips a beat with each reading of Lycaon. Impermanence is what can only be described as a lyrical masterpiece.

Diane Narraway

BORN OF THE FOAM

Beloved, you are in all of us invoked

In sweet memory tied to a devotee's
hand

Where lovers breathe intoxication

Desirous of seed to flower lush
necessity

How stirred you are within our
tangled heat

Engaged beneath your soaking crown.

Here mustered is the drug of scent,

Clamouring un-born from the shell

Split open to the taste of a frenzied
joy—

As itself eternity—the milk of deep
night

And harboured there, o Holy
Aphrodite

Lies divine your vital promiscuity.

DECONSTRUCTION

I loved you
in the wake of monuments
crashed
in their force

like a good thing
cascading down
toward the dirty
distilled light of forsaken time.

This is the axiom:
sing me each corner,
spread my latitude
before any truth.

I am alone the central pillar—
the grace of each fountain;
each wonder of bold youth—
a rose of the unfurled …

THE FALL

The adversary
is a God on earth
who revels in shattered vessels
undistinguished from the flame
and the hand that gave man fire—

torn they will say from the cosmos
and slung toward the soil—

claimed by the
first sister of our transgression
ave! our liberator coils
about Her
frame!

And the mark is made
as the body emulates
first of passion,
for it was ordained
that man was made
greater for His fall.

Here and within,
to cede Man the wealth of the Earth
once turned are his own
heels on heaven.

ARMENIACA

She was, they say, the first woman
ever to sing

high in mountains, deep into glen and
forest

out into volumed glades she would
roam

haunting the lush streams of far-
wondrous Asia

enchanting all who chanced her way.

Dumbstruck she would render
helpless

many men who'd asked to revel her…

until the God of the forest one dawn
gave chase

and cornered her to have of his wild
way.

In his enrapture she did resist as he
spake:

'Why will you not let me carry you
away?

into my meadow bed, where you can indulge me

your many duties, make me

understand your mystery?

Within the luscious home of your being

there will come the senses

fulfilled into the nameless...

daggered into the pattern of your rivulet–

whole at one within your estuary

my lightning seed to settle into flower...

You, my love, work sweet not sour

on the end of my sweet wit...'

And she replied as best she could

'If I am yours, I belong to you and you alone

and the world is in need of my sultry tone.

So, there it is, I must remain free to wander

and give my love-song to all
mankind.'

The God left his reply astray
to move in on his prey, to clutch
her into him, he approached
as day chases night
she backed away.

As she stood, startled at the God's
passion
his teeth now lathering saliva
hastening toward her harried form,
she hurried away from him.

But it was there, underneath the
Armeniaca tree
the Father of All Song intervened...

He pulled her into a stern trunk—
where her hands became branches
her veins clotted sudden with sap
away from the randy God of the
gnarling thicket...

Some say it was Orpheus himself

who saved her music for Man,

but nevertheless, salvation
transformed

great sadness was known across the
land.

Then many generations down

a wanderer would stumble upon that
same tree—

fine maker of woodwind vessels—

in joy he would carve from this
apricot tree

into the reed he would breathe divine

and in the lament of the wind's kiss

she lived again in the wailing of her
loss

forever in the voice of the Duduk.

DOWRY

A grey hand
withered like a widow's

handing over that, which is taken
left in emptiness

with a void for a womb
where flowers once grew

now two torches follow
the anguish...

And the King of Hell is left

alone
a mother will dwell
on the law

of father over to son,
here Her world is unborn

o mother of the crop withhold
how you withheld your child...

until she became,
Kore unto the world.

CLYTAEMNESTRA

Too many years have passed dear
child,

since last you were adored by these
mother's eyes,

when the wind sail rose above our
own

flesh and blood, I will avenge with my
own hand

for the ruin of my heart—
a villain,

your beast of a father that his fleet
would not stand

immemorial for the paltry breeze—

he made it so my sweet Iphigenia—

given unto the winds to appease of
Artemis

bound in the cloth and gagged for the
knife's vile work

what pity fell upon Aulis

and how your sacrifice would set
such pitiless course.

I speak to a ghost no longer at my
side

but always in my heart, sweet girl

though grown as cold and hard as the winter;

deceived and vanished child.

I remember too well the disbelief, your swooning;

your dismay as life slowly seeped

before the knife ever pierced of your form,

your eyes alone they gnawed

at each commander witness there, you laboured for voice,

struggled to define

this father's debt to an end that he would not compromise.

Many of his men would remember your voice

as young in spirit, full of dash and harmony

and whilst they many did weep as their shame compelled!

only I would contend with a mother's grief.

Stood before your image,

I know I have seen your maiden tears

trickle from the lifeless stone–

adorned with your favourite rosemary

how scent enamours you, precious
child

from the meadows of my memory.

WOUND

The sea retreats,
the moon tilts back on herself
as the purple sky embraces of the still

even hope turns back
the murmurs in the breeze
for the song was sung so sadly.

Such anguish and betrayal...
the leaves must fall to the dirt
alone to breathe Her within

and begin they not feud
with such caressing hand
that will vanish,

along with Her mercy
to hush the Earth in
a wounding sleep.

SON OF IAPETUS

What testimony I should give to the
Earth...

Bound, rallied to the rock to which I
am priest

To all that speak my venerating name

Prometheus bold Titan I am found

At liberty within these firm-held
chains

I am fixed upon a point of no return

No longer am I that fashioner of men,
or

So, I am told harsh lipped at the rein

To He that keeps me woefully
betrayed

In the hope that I should beckon to
reason

Within a world of this frustrating, no
appeasement

Shall come delivered the fruit of the
unrestrained

No more to sully the adamantine
wedge

In that visceral power challenged and
tame

Zeus'–you who have made mine own
deliverance

From a scoundrel low to a martyr's
edge

The longer glory held is held in mine
own pain.

What martyrdom you seek for man, I
gauge

The countenance that you betray,
aloft

Olympus, power is tantamount on
high

Low lies the gully that comes my bliss

Mine altar of defiance paid by
visitations:

Of heralds come nigh to the gnaw at
the conscience

Splayed, more so beguiled by wonders
of this Earth

Whom keep me company at the
anguished hearth

Here you should be witness first, not
last, Zeus?

To thine own tyrant cloaked in miseries harsh

For he that would not carry the yoke

Nor be pummelled under the lightning stroke

I am not he that was born of the clay unfathomed

Some poor lonely decree, no shadow am I!

No gutless phantasm, I am Man

To walk with torch withheld by thee

My trick circumvents your power, deceived.

To what then Zeus, of mine incursion wrought?

You think of me some lowly thwart to your design;

Belittle me at your behest, it is your kind

To lower me down confined to that prison in the depth

Enabled more a scapegoat, confess to power

Granted sly a trickster I—no benefactor less

Your Strength and Violence may caress

My effigy upon this desolating crag– near Oceanus

O makers of man no less unbound is thine hand

That cries in tones of freedom tied held

Sound in irons warped by the brother —God of Fire!

Clasp it firmer still, the detriment your own

Zeus, I will never been alone in the wilderness

The clay fashions better in this, your abyss

Hardened in the sorrowful nags of constraint

Inspired by the kisses of breathing saints

Loving more in this suffering of mine

I defiant stand, Prometheus.

FAE

Conundrum of the midnight

hour-mist of the ancient breeze

of the sea's salt stroke and the wild
wind

that skirts the coppice edge...

come the skirmish of these autumn
leaves

o'er the bridge of my startled menace

unto the dawn; safe from the low-folk

whose games grace sullen earth their
grin.

For I have walked throughout the
night

led by wonder and awe astray

round and round in a pretty circle...

LYCAON

Beneath the sun's just light

he will descend irreversible

Father Jove caught him out in the end

for serving that abomination.

Lycaon deserved his plight

his every agonising shift of shape

for the shade of his slaughtered boy;

corrupting father

scorn of blood

he will writhe

the unendurable

carved into the mortal flesh

his mouth skin contorting

breaching hairs

catch the gargling spittle and froth,

his two legs groan into four

as hand becomes paw

Dike will be stood aloft:
his vanishing into time

FREEZE

Writing in the porcelain dusk
my entry of which I am proud

into this still world through which I
then became suspended

in a pool that did not ripple
more in the grey light

tight
unforgiving like fog into

moveless still:
 life's transparency

clear as the sin
froze in its own winter negative

its doom-frame given
unto crystallizing damp,
Aeon of dour fragment!
give leniency, I am...

hung between these

midnight waves of my emotion.

KOUROS

Give the mortal plane your chariot
song

then turn abide the waiting ear,

be tried and enter the labyrinth

merged with its own opposition

the frontier where all is one—

stop all time—

here your age is measured in
breathing

desire, longing held

in the beating heart.

You have yet to escape in death

yet to have left of life

hear now

the hiss of the great God in his lair

proven though you are in the flesh

by vigour, Kouros come...

KALLIOPE ON THE DEATH OF HER SON

Toward the world that is waiting for
you

memory sings along branches downstream

when you are gone, we have exhaled

in your presence, then withered

some flowers will bloom for just that
day

but you will flow forever

in the basin of a marble heart

blest mausoleum of life

sculpted in the dance of their order

their precision—

the Sun will out-blaze the weary
Bacchoi...

reach harmony with your father,
Apollo.

Now scattered like the God you used
to serve—

your own affirmation in death—

immortal life and Mother of
Remembrance

infinite

eternal as the seven-stringed breath

walking away is your form...

You are the music—wanderer

a blue-cloak that sways in the breeze.

INTENSITY

A chiselled memory

retched into time

from a wish corrupted, desire
sublimed

like a day-dream turned.

Smouldering

left the breathless bone...

unreconciled in the beatless heart,

drowned out in ashes.

THE PRECIPICE

What great work of art could not be
fathomed in a day?

How long should the soul withstand
the Muses' dazzling dart?

The haunting ghost of Rilke's
February now long past.

I invite ecstasy aboard my own
incarnate form

Alea iacta est ... I cross the Rubicon

And I may die a sick man for the die
already cast

I am flanked by many bodies of
treason

I know the truth is my own obscured
in mist

I ask all the forces of my nature for
this

Yet fractured easily, how deftly
assailed is sense—

How much I have maligned the
matter

To tear worthless flesh from the arc of
each season.

Invisible spirit, O gathering angel wound!

Ripe bud of consciousness; phantom to the self!

Will the word come to me as we merge?

Shall the hymn breathe its last breath crowned absurd?

They tell me, these entities of unseen layer

How riderless the rider must ride on...

Through the maelstrom of image, sensation, unreason...

Transcendence I think but to think is to be

Mere scribe; chained within some safe oblivion:

As silence refines all speech there oft is a flower

Too soon in blossom, besieged by calculating frost

Of petals once withered, unclaimed they turn into stone

Am I never to flow in the Father's celestial stream?

Should I not know by now dank caverns of the Goddess Earth?

Shall moments of eternity but perish utterly?

And yet I sit on the roof of the sun, momentarily

Over short meagre time exalt this depth in being...

And forge my river here, to cast downstream unto the world.

REMEMBER IN THE TIMES TO COME

In the shoal of our worth
we gouge into love,
bite the cud of failure,
bless each win.

All dragged under
the kicking sun we pour
the honest rattle of our faint mention
to others among,
beneath vague stars
we become...

Remember this in times to come

we will play like children
beneath the austere chapels
and clap instead for the maelstrom—

proud accomplices wielding rebel tone
and strife

for tomorrow

and all of its thunder.

IMPERMANENCE

It is impermanence, this battlefield...

A lowly waging master known as Time

His worn shell unclasping of its life-
yield

Exist there ... now a husk blown in
rumour

Travelling through the seams of that
duress

Like iron smelting down ancient blood
stream.

Necessity will render rich those
narrow corridors

Where Fate once made us weep such
colours

Stricken grey from the form that
turns us

Flowers into old age displayed in our
Chance

We reminisce on the Fortune, wear
garlands

Only to mark the memory ripe for
dissolution.

THE DEAD RETURN IN EARNEST

One day there will be
poetry on the Caucasus again

blood mingled with dialect
music from the caves—
your being shall rise after
it cascades into nothingness.

There begins the alchemy
in the thunder of the rebel
in the seed of departing soul
within all-gift is both birth and decay

O Flower of Immortality
as the seasons pound the memory!

I must be again...

THE END

Ingram Content Group UK Ltd.
Milton Keynes UK
UKHW052121130323
418475UK00012B/132

9 781914 071935